Academic Life Coaching Workbook College Edition

John Andrew Williams

1.0 Coach Training Guide
Copyright 2020 by John Andrew Williams.

A Publication of
Coach Training EDU
3605 NE US Grant Place
Portland, Oregon 97212

January 31, 2020

Table of Contents

Welcome to ALC

Congratulations on taking a big step. Working with an Academic Life Coach while in college is one of the most important investments you can make with your time and energy. You are at a turning point in your life. Your decisions and the path that you take will put you on a trajectory that will influence the rest of your life.

Life coaching helps you define and clarify what you really want and design actions and habits to achieve it. With its roots in sports psychology, life coaching takes the same principles an elite athlete would use to be at the top of his or her game and applies it to life. It's a profession that doesn't diagnose problems or provide interventions. Instead, it provides an arena for you to explore ideas and craft perspectives that lead to your taking effective action.

The most pervasive myth surrounding life coaching – or any helping profession – is that seeking support is a sign of weakness; an admission that something is wrong or broken. The truth is the exact opposite. Working with a coach is an indication of strength. The best athletes in the world work with multiple coaches. The most successful executives have coaches. People at the highest levels of any profession understand the value of coaching, and now it's your chance to experience the benefits. But before we embark on the coaching journey, let's take a look at a few key points in coaching's history.

Laying the foundation for life coaching and positive psychology was Timothy Galloway's *Inner Game of Tennis*, a breakthrough novel written in 1977. The book gave tennis its reputation for being a "mental game" where staying calm and focused were keys to being successful. Galloway also paved the way for sport coaches to address the inner world of competing with as much energy as the outward display of skill and technique.

In the 1980's Olympic athletes from many different countries pushed sports psychology further with advanced visualization techniques and positive framing. The 1980's also saw a significant increase in mentoring and leadership development programs in the business and corporate world. Such a trend accelerated in following years with organizations supporting life coaching and positive psychology being formally founded in the late 1990's.

In the mid-2000's, I pursued my coach training and started to incorporate life coaching concepts specifically to academia and the student experience. Out of that work came the concepts and foundation of the Academic Life Coaching Program, which maps several concepts of life coaching to the student experience.

Mapping the 4 Cornerstones

Over the past few decades, student persistence and engagement have been the topics of dozens of studies. Those studies suggest that having a few key traits significantly boosts your chances of successfully graduating from college and pursuing a fulfilling and effective career beyond. Those four traits are: having an accurate understanding of one's capabilities, feeling a sense of belonging, adopting a growth mindset, and an ability to create sustainable systems.

While you work with an Academic Life Coach, you will naturally address these areas. However, having a map in hand is useful to understand the four cornerstones that form the foundation of a successful academic experience. Using core coaching concepts such as the Making Distinctions tool and assessment tools such as the Wheel of Life, we can create a diagram that maps each of these areas. The first is a distinction between the inner world – your inner dialogue, beliefs, and emotions – and your external world – your actions, relationships, and community. The second is a distinction between your academic (or professional) life and your personal (or private) life. If you map out those two distinctions, you'll create a diagram that addresses the four cornerstones of your life experience.

Mapping the Four Cornerstones

	Internal	*External*
Personal	**Knowledge of Self** Self-Talk Briefs & Assumptions	**Community** Friendships Relationships
Academic	**Perspectives on Work & Study** Mindsets about Academic Ability Styles of Motivation	**Habits & Systems** Results & Feedback Experiences & Learning

Let's look at each of these cornerstones in turn and how each lines up the four factors research which has shown to make a difference in determining a student's success in college and beyond.

First Cornerstone: Self-Knowledge

The first part of the program focuses on increasing your self-awareness and building your fluency with your thoughts, emotions, and habits. We each have an internal language and dialogue made up of empowering or limiting beliefs, assumptions, and perspectives. When you learn how to speak and interpret this internal language, you will soon discover what actions you need to take to be more fulfilled and effective, and less stressed. This segment of the program is a constant train of "Aha!" moments that build interpersonal skills and a strong foundation of personal fluency.

Growth in self-knowledge is moving from the question "Am I good enough?" to "Who am I and what are my strengths?"

Second Cornerstone: Community

The second factor is your ability to create a support system and build relationships and a community. The friendships you make in college will last a lifetime. Understanding and cultivating those relationships is an important part of living a fulfilled and effective life. Being a good friend, while learning when and how to ask for help effectively, is an important skill that leads to creating a network and community of people who are committed to supporting you and providing help when you need it most. In time, you will also give back and help others; and really, this kind of giving and receiving is a crucial element to fully participating in your community.

Growth is moving from "Do I belong?" to "How can I build community?"

Third Cornerstone: Mindsets and Perspectives

From the point-of-view of a growth mindset, success and failure are merely feedback on how you are doing. Neither changes the fact that you are still going to put in work and go after mastering your subject or craft. This cornerstone looks at your willingness to delay gratification, find an empowering perspective, manage setbacks, and do the necessary work. From such a perspective, if you keep moving forward and putting in effort, success is going to happen. Failure is going to happen too. Both are useful for learning, and if you are not having failures along the way, you are not trying hard enough nor will you achieve as many meaningful successes in your life.

Growth is moving from asking "Is the work worth it?" to "What work is worth it?"

Fourth Cornerstone: Habits and Systems

The final factor is developing sustainable systems to get the grades you want while managing stress. The systems you create are an outward manifestation of the inner work – the perspectives, mindsets, and clarity – you've crafted. The interplay between the inner world of perspectives and the actions you take begin to form your habits which leads to feedback: the failure or success you experience. When you start to connect your mindset and work with outside possibilities, you start to create a future path for yourself that goes beyond school to starting a career. Once you gain clarity on your career, school gains even more meaning. As you continue to take steps toward that reality, your professional life begins.

Growth is moving from asking "Can I succeed?" to "How do I succeed?"

Elements of a Coaching Session

While coaching concepts can influence even a short, ten-second conversation or influence an entire classroom, the typical coaching session lasts between 30 to 60 minutes. Each session has certain elements that are helpful for you to know so that you can get as much as you can out of the conversation.

WHAT

The main elements of a coaching session are: a quick check-in on previous action steps, setting the current coaching session agenda, exploration, and crafting a plan of action for you to take between coaching sessions. Of these elements, crafting a useful session agenda is the most important. It serves as a foundation and focal point for all the other work that you will do with your coach. If you have a strong session agenda – which can change mid-point in a session – you have a strong container to frame the following exploration. Much of your coach's training has looked at how to help you craft a useful and powerful agenda for each session.

WHY

So much of coaching is designed to help you become more proactive in your life. The more prepared you are in coming to a coaching session with something to focus on, and what specifically you want to get out of the session, the more value you will receive from the coaching.

As you experience coaching and bring coaching concepts and actions plans into your life, you will experience the world differently. Situations will arise that will make you reflect on your coaching sessions and you will bring more complex questions and agendas to your sessions. Embrace the growth and actively seek out what you want to know. Your confidence will increase as you push the edges of your understanding and deepen the insights you want to explore. Coaching works. You can trust the process.

HOW

In the following section there is space for session notes. You will find space for a session agenda, notes, action steps, and reflection. To prepare for a session, you're invited to fill out the reflection prompts (What worked well? and What did not?) as well as write down initial ideas on what you want to focus on for your upcoming session.

During the session, your coach will most likely have a suggestion for an exercise to use. You will find a description and explanation of coaching concepts following the coaching notes. You're welcome to read the explanations ahead of time and ask your coach about any specific exercises you might want to use in your session.

Near the end of each session, you'll have an opportunity to design the next action step for you to take. A useful perspective on those action steps is to consider them mini-experiments designed to create more understanding as well as opportunities to increase your productivity and stamina. So much value is created between sessions in the coaching process when you take consistent action steps to experience even deeper insights.

Session Notes

Date:

Session Agenda:

Notes:

Agreed-upon action steps:

Debrief (to be filled out during the week or at the beginning of the next session)

What worked?

What did not work?

Session Notes

Date:

Session Agenda:

Notes:

Agreed-upon action steps:

Debrief (to be filled out during the week or at the beginning of the next session)

What worked?

What did not work?

Session Notes

Date:

Session Agenda:

Notes:

Agreed-upon action steps:

Debrief (to be filled out during the week or at the beginning of the next session)

What worked?

What did not work?

Session Notes

Date:

Session Agenda:

Notes:

Agreed-upon action steps:

Debrief (to be filled out during the week or at the beginning of the next session)

What worked?

What did not work?

Session Notes

Date:

Session Agenda:

Notes:

Agreed-upon action steps:

Debrief (to be filled out during the week or at the beginning of the next session)

What worked?

What did not work?

Session Notes

Date:

Session Agenda:

Notes:

Agreed-upon action steps:

Debrief (to be filled out during the week or at the beginning of the next session)

What worked?

What did not work?

Session Notes

Date:

Session Agenda:

Notes:

Agreed-upon action steps:

Debrief (to be filled out during the week or at the beginning of the next session)

What worked?

What did not work?

Session Notes

Date:

Session Agenda:

Notes:

Agreed-upon action steps:

Debrief (to be filled out during the week or at the beginning of the next session)

What worked?

What did not work?

Coaching Exercises

In the section that follows, you will find descriptions of coaching exercises. These exercises are not meant to be completed in any particular order. Please discuss any exercises you would like to try with your coach. The more you take control of your coaching sessions, the more you'll gain from the process.

Design the Client-Coach Alliance

At some point near the beginning of your coaching relationship, your coach will invite you to offer suggestions, requests, and ideas on how a coaching session can work the best for you.

WHAT

A designed alliance is a mindful relationship centered on empowering you as a client to ask for the exact kind and style of coaching you want in order to be successful. It's an opportunity for you to give you coach feedback and make requests so you feel eager to meet with your coach and confident you'll get what you need out of each coaching session.

WHY

When you directly address what, why, and how you want to communicate, you eliminate many assumptions that could get in the way of deeper insights. When you open up frank and direct channels of communication, you empower the relationship and create a high degree of safety in a coaching session. Consciously designing such a relationship puts the coaching process on a powerful foundation.

HOW

Throughout coaching, we have the opportunity to design the relationship in a way that best serves you. To do so, it is helpful to consider the following questions:

1. What best motivates you?

2. What requests do you have?

3. What do you think I should know as your coach?

4. What is (or is not) working so far?

5. How will you know that this coaching has been successful?

Wheel of Life

When you're feeling like you need an overall assessment of how things are going, or an overall big picture perspective, the Wheel of Life Exercise is perfect.

WHAT

The *Wheel of Life* is a popular coaching exercise that gives you a quick overview of your life. It's a quick assessment of your current level of satisfaction in each area that also provides a visual of how different areas of your life are connected.

WHY

A quick overview gives you a new perspective as well as an opportunity to focus on an area of your life which you otherwise wouldn't address.

HOW

Use the diagram of a wheel on the following page as a starting point. Rate your current level of satisfaction with each of the areas on the wheel. Your coach will take it from there.

Questions to consider:

1. **Looking at your wheel, what jumps out at you?**

2. **If you were to choose just one wedge and do one action to increase that number from a 7 to an 8 (for instance), what would that action be?**

Save your wheels. I do this exercise for myself about once every three months and note the date. It is useful to look back and see the difference consistent actions can make in the long-run. This exercise is designed to ensure your life is balanced and a tool to remind you how far you have come.

Date:

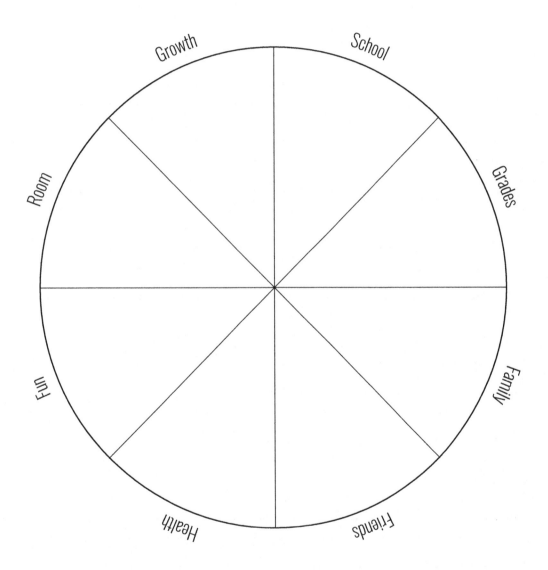

Well-Designed Actions

When you find yourself frustrated with too many goals, or you've heard the word goal too many times, it's time to look at crafting Well-Designed Actions instead.

WHAT

The *well-designed* part of the exercise title refers to crafting a task that focuses energy and attention in such a way that boosts intrinsic motivation. The action part of a well-designed action refers to thinking in terms of systems, not merely in terms of work and reward.

A Well-Designed Action meets the following four criteria.

- **It's stated in the positive.**

- **Getting started and completing the action relies entirely on you.**

- **The action is large enough to excite but small enough not to overwhelm.**

- **The action is measurable.**

WHY

When people think about life coaching and improving their life, goals is often the first word that comes to mind. On one hand, having goals is great. However, the word is overused, and the mere mention of goals often causes stress levels to go up. The concept of having 'SMART' goals can sometimes be useful, but the process of setting goals and then trying hard to achieve them (often by doing the same actions, just harder) usually leads to frustration.

The biggest virtue of the Well-Designed Action is that it empowers you to take full control of the success or failure of the outcome. So much of our lives falls outside of our control. A Well-Designed Action starts with a goal, or a desire, but then obsessively focuses the action on only what you can control. Such a focus frees up mental and emotional energy to pour into those actions that are most likely to lead to success.

For example, it is impossible to control the grade that you may get on an essay, as it is ultimately up to the instructor what grade you receive. A well-designed action, on the other hand, encourages you to focus on the actual process of writing your paper. The grade becomes feedback. Ironically, not focusing on the grade as a goal, but instead focusing on becoming a better writer, is the best way for you to get your top grade.

HOW

The first step is to start with a goal or a desire, then work backwards to make sure that your action plan falls into this criteria:

1. **Your plan is stated in the positive.**

   You are focusing on what you want rather than on what you don't want.

2. **You can completely control the start, process, and finish of the action.**

   In other words, you are not relying on outside forces to determine your success.

3. **Your plan is ambitious enough to be exciting yet small enough to be manageable.**

   Finding the balance and learning from previous weeks requires a process of constant refinement and planning.

4. **You can measure your actions and outcome.**

Looking at ways to measure your success makes the process tangible.

Examples

Goal: To get all A's

Well-Designed Action: To study for all of my tests for one hour or more two days before the test date.

Goal: To not get a bad grade

Well-Designed Action: To write in my planner each class, and if I don't have any homework I will write "no homework"

Core Motivation

Sometimes an idea can change your life. Core Motivation offers a number of insights that hold such a promise. When you want to get to the next level, Core Motivation is for you.

WHAT

Core Motivation is a tool based on the Enneagram. *Ennea* in ancient Greek means *nine*. *Gram* means *drawing*. The Enneagram is literally a nine point drawing describing nine different personality types connected in different ways. One aspect of Core Motivation that makes it so powerful is that it's both descriptive and prescriptive. It gives you insights into your character traits, points a path forward, and offers suggestions for your personal growth.

WHY

Finding what really motivates you is a tremendous benefit in helping overcome challenges and doing the work that needs to be done. It is also a tool to develop your self-awareness. It can help you gain a better understanding of how to take advantage of your personality strengths and manage your weaknesses. The tool points to the natural strengths of your core motivation as well as potential blind spots that limit and hinder your success.

Any personality system faces the challenge of being descriptive without boxing in the richness of your uniqueness. The concern is valid. However, Core Motivation posits that everyone is a bit of every type. The difference is that you will most likely gravitate toward one or two of the types, while leaving open the possibility for you to identify with other types as well.

HOW

To find your core motivation, read the nine paragraphs below. Everyone has a little of each type. In different parts of our lives we can rely on different motivations. A few of these will seem to fit you best. Find the one or two that fit best. After you determine your style, your coach will help you learn more details about your core motivation and integrate what you have learned into the Academic Life Coaching Program.

Core Motivation Types

Type One: The Perfectionist

I strive for things to be perfect and in place. If I am passionate about something, I work really hard and spend a lot of time on it. I want other things around me to be perfect, but I am mostly hard on myself. I am very critical of the things I do, and I am very disappointed in myself when I make a mistake. I often have a lot of priorities on my plate, but I just want to improve my life and the lives of others. Often, people follow my lead, and I am comfortable in that leadership capacity. Whatever I have to do, it has to be done right, and I will do what it takes to get there. Others might say I am intense or too serious at times, but I just like to be focused and I would rather relax when the work is done.

Type Two: The Helper

What really drives me is my ability to help others. I love doing things for somebody, especially if I know they will appreciate it. I feel like I know how best to help people because it is usually easy for me to determine their wants and needs. It might seem like I try too hard or am controlling at times, but it is just because I want to help in the best way. I get satisfaction out of putting others before myself, though sometimes it takes its toll when I do not focus on my own needs. I like when others recognize that I am there for them, and I usually have a difficult time saying no. I also place a huge emphasis on relationships. I give a lot of myself in hopes that others will recognize what I have given, and in turn will respect me for that. At the end of the day, I hope that the people I help will be there for me when necessary.

Type Three: The Doer

I want to be the best I can be at what I do. Goals are important to me, and I work hard at achieving them. I feel very successful when I meet my goals, and I want others to respect me for it. My mind works rather quickly, and sometimes I can get irritable if something or someone seems to be working too slowly. Though I am personally competitive, I can also do well on a team and am well liked. I want to make a good impression on people, and I care about how others view me. When I have a really passionate goal, I know just what to do to achieve it and stay motivated. I prefer to do only the things I am good at.

Type Four: The Artist

I like to express my emotions, and I want others to understand me for who I am. I consider myself genuine and unique. I am constantly seeking more in terms of my life, and I try to evaluate and consider what is missing. I do not like to be misunderstood. Sometimes people might mistake me for being dramatic or caring too much, but really I just want to express exactly how I feel. I like to get to know others on a deeper level and form real connections. I am passionate about feelings, and I want to accurately reveal myself to others.

Type Five: The Thinker

I love being the expert. Before I delve into something, I want to know as much as I can. I do not like to be wrong or corrected, which is why if I do not know something, I would rather not say it. I am happy to argue my points for what I believe is right, but if the facts do not support my idea, I will reconsider my idea. I often thrive on alone time, and I like to think about my past experiences. I am pretty independent, and I do not want to have to rely or depend on someone else. I crave information and knowledge, and I am not shy in a group setting, where I can speak up and say what I know and express what I want. Overall, I am a simple person, and my life is rather straightforward.

Type Six: The Friend

I like to be prepared for the worst. Often I envision worst-case scenarios so that I know just what to do in case they actually happen. I have a creative imagination and a somewhat odd sense of humor. I can be unsure of people in authority, especially if I do not trust them. Once I trust someone and have explored an idea, I will be very loyal. When it comes to new ideas, the first thing that usually comes to mind is what could go wrong. I would rather think it through before accepting it at face value. I am not much of a follower, especially when it comes to ideas, because I can easily pick out why I disagree with it.

Type Seven: The Optimist

I enjoy life at a fast pace. I like to create many options for myself and future plans. I keep many options open. I shy away from negative emotion, and I hate feeling bored or trapped with my life. If I am upset over something, I do not want to dwell on it. Sometimes I will get really excited over something rather quickly, but then eventually I will get bored with it and forget about it or drop it. Often, I will start things that do not quite get finished. At the same time, I am very optimistic, and I believe life is a ride that is meant to be enjoyed. When I have several options that I can choose from, I have a hard time deciding because I want them all.

Type Eight: The Defender

I like to be in control as much as possible. I am very blunt and honest because I want things to be clear. It frustrates me when I feel like someone is conniving or unfair. At times, I might seem controlling, but I just want to take charge and keep things going smoothly. I try to hide my weaknesses because I feel vulnerable when someone else knows what they are. That being said, I think we should still recognize our weaknesses and do something about them. I would rather get something done on my own than be told what to do, which is why I sometimes have a hard time following orders from authority. I will not always respect a person of authority upfront, but when I do, I am much more willing to follow directions from them.

Type Nine: The Peacemaker

I like things to be peaceful and happy. I tend to avoid conflict and confrontation. Sometimes I cannot even recognize exactly what I want, so I just go with the flow, especially in group settings. When I do know what I want, I might still agree with someone even if it goes against that. I might get angry at myself, but I do not like getting angry at other people, or when people are angry at each other. I have a kind heart, and I know it can be taken advantage of. When I really need to, I know how to stand up for myself. I am good at seeing multiple sides to a situation, both pros and cons.

Challenges to Personal Growth	Exercises that aid personal growth
Type 1: The Perfectionist	
Being too hard on myself. Being too serious. Not taking time for myself for fun and pure enjoyment. Demanding perfection and not accepting every part of myself.	Improvisation and activities like improv are outstanding for 1's. Improv activities let 1's act without getting stuck in their thoughts. Taking time out of the day for fun and laughter.
Type 2: The Helper	
Doing so much for others that I forget to take care of my needs. Becoming too involved in relationships. Becoming demanding when I am not recognized.	Write out what you want for each area of your life and determine clearly what balance you want to achieve. Set aside time to treat yourself as you would treat another person.
Type 3: The Doer	
Realizing that your worth is who you are, not what you have accomplished. Sacrificing personal relationships for the sake of a goal.	Relax your focus on success and put your focus on what would fulfill you. Clarify your values and what's really important to you.
Type 4: The Artist	
Over identifying with emotion, especially sad emotion, without moving into action. Resisting change if it is not dramatic. Feeling unworthy. Focusing too much on yourself.	Practice changing perspectives and choosing those perspectives that empower you to get what you really want. Create a positive vision of your future life.
Type 5: The Thinker	
Over-analyzing and being stubborn. Avoiding people or opportunities that seem overwhelming. Being very private. Not moving into action.	Meditation. Especially short meditation during the day to check in with your emotions. When considering an action, go for it.

Type 6: The Friend	
Not trusting yourself or others. Thinking about worst-case scenarios. Wanting to keep knowing more before making a decision. Doubt.	Check in with fear. Practice identifying perspectives and choosing positive ones to move forward. Positive affirmations.
Type 7: The Optimist	
Thinking that something you don't have will be better than what you already have. Avoiding pain and not meeting responsibilities. Being distracted from bigger goals.	Clarify a mission statement and take small action steps to accomplish it. Meditation is very important to 7's. Exercise discipline.
Type 8: The Defender	
Being stubborn. Denying weakness and sensitivity. Fighting any attempt to be controlled and trying to control others. Acting in ways that make success harder to accomplish.	Focus on the gift that you can give to others. Listen closely to others and practice empathy. Resist being stubborn and constantly resisting others.
Type 9: The Peacemaker	
Ignoring problems and trying to be comfortable always. Not meeting problems when they first start and avoiding conflict at any cost. Not knowing what you really want.	Clarify a mission statement and commit to taking small action steps. Practice asserting yourself and saying no to small things. Refuse to be passive aggressive. Instead, be assertive.

Challenges and Exercises for Personal Growth

My primary core motivation:

Challenges most apt to you:

How you know you are doing well:

Exercises for personal growth:

Academic Thinking Styles

When you are looking for a systematic way to organize your studies or you are getting increasingly frustrated with your academic results even though you are putting in the work, Academic Thinking Styles are for you.

What

There are three main Academic Thinking Styles. The first is looking for *what*. A *what* thinking style looks for names, dates, details, categories, and definitions. The second is seeking after *why*. A *why* thinking style looks for the deeper reasons, the underpinnings, and implications of the concept. The third thinking style, *how*, looks for the steps, the process, and the paths forward. Each of these thinking styles plays a crucial role in academic learning. Everyone uses all three nearly simultaneously, but as learners we tend to favor one or two over the others.

Why

Understanding the Academic Thinking Styles helps you seek out and organize information in a more effective way. Using thinking styles is a tool to help you understand your own style as well as become aware of potential blind-spots in your studying.

When you know your thinking style, you will know your strength and you will also know what thinking styles you need to develop. Ideally, you are equally comfortable with all three thinking styles. It helps to get into the habit of taking notes in a what/why/how style and to include each thinking style in your writing.

How

Your Academic Life Coach will provide a lot of valuable experience to help you determine your thinking style. Sometimes your style is readily apparent. Sometimes it is tough to determine. The key is to recognize the kinds of questions you find yourself asking when trying to learn something new. You can find your Academic Thinking Style by reading the paragraphs below and seeing which one or two matches you best.

What Thinking Style

What thinkers love details and want to know the names, definitions, facts, and more about the material itself. *What* thinkers may put a copious number of facts in an essay, and put hours of work into their writing, but get frustrated when teachers want more analysis and assign a low grade. (In other words, the teachers want to know more than just the facts and see a balance of thinking styles in an essay.) *What* thinkers assume that if they can know all the correct facts, and are knowledgeable about the details of a situation, the cause (*why*) or sequence (*how*) is apparent.

Why Thinking Style

Why thinkers want to understand the reasons behind the action. Detail is somewhat important, but not as important as knowing someone's motivation to do something or the cause of something happening. These kinds of learners tend to drive teachers wild, especially in a subject like math. *Why* thinkers assume that if they can understand the causes behind something, they then know all the important facts.

How Thinking Style

How thinkers want to understand how they can do something or how it happened. To a *how* thinker, most details are not that important, but the essential details are paramount. When writing, *how* thinkers tend to summarize or retell the event *from a particular point-of-view*. As a result, a how thinker's papers tend to be light on synopsis and analysis and make the reader work to fill in many of the details and analysis. *How* thinkers assume that the reasons are obvious and the details are usually superfluous. Yet, if someone knows how to do something, all the other pieces of knowledge will fall into place.

Applying the Thinking Styles

Each Thinking Style is a channel or method of thought. Each is valid and important. Similar to a learning style, one of the goals of thinking styles is to become proficient at each style and know which style might be your weak point. If you know, for instance, that you are a *how* thinker, you may want to take more time focusing on specific definitions or names when studying. If you are a *what* thinker, you may want to spend more time looking at the analysis and the reasons behind an action. If you are a *why* thinker, it may be worthwhile to spend more time on the names and definitions as well as the specific methods for solving a problem.

The key to using thinking styles is to become comfortable with each style, and to make sure that when you are studying you understand the concept from each of the three angles.

1. **What are the details and definitions?**

2. **Why did it happen this way? Why does it work?**

3. **How did it happen? How can I do it?**

Exercises for Building your Thinking Styles:

- **Take notes that you would usually take in class.**

   Then, when reviewing your notes, code them into What, Why, and How for each major concept. If you cannot find a Why or How, that may be a good question to ask your professor or teacher's assistant.

- **Practice writing paragraphs that address each of the three questions.**

   Students often find themselves favoring one thinking style, which leads to writing that is either filled with too many details and little analysis, or a summary of what happened without letting the reader know what the main topic is and why it's important. By addressing each of the three thinking styles, in turn, you ensure that you will begin to write outstanding paragraphs and papers.

- **Pay attention to the kinds of questions each professor asks and the kinds of information your professor is giving in class.**

   Is your professor fond of names, dates, and details? If so, then he or she is probably a *what* thinker. Does your professor like to delve into the possible reasons why something happens? Then he or she tends toward *why* thinking. Does he or she spend a lot of time going step-by-step through the problem or section? Then he or she is probably a *how* thinker. Knowing what Thinking Style your professor uses can help you craft appropriate questions during class time.

Science of Learning

Learning is your ability to gain new knowledge and experience. Your fulfillment and success rely to a large degree on how fast and efficiently you learn new skills. When you want to apply the latest science of learning to leverage insights and try out what has been shown to work best, this section is for you.

WHAT

This section looks at studies on learning and identifies the most useful exercises for you to learn efficiently and effectively. Each method – from self-testing to engaging as many senses as possible – relies on you being proactive. You need to actively seek out the knowledge for the sake of learning, rather than doing homework or studying just for the grade.

WHY

Learning is a natural skill. Babies and young children learn rapidly because they are not afraid to make mistakes. The same fearlessness and obliviousness to making mistakes also applies to adults, but grades create a culture where mistakes are not appreciated and playfulness is not encouraged. It is safer to stick with tried-and-true strategies. As you go through the Academic Life Coaching Program, your coach will help you tap into the resourceful playfulness which is optimal for learning.

The grades you earn are not a reflection of your intelligence. Grades are a reflection of the system and habits you use to learn. Change your learning habits, and you will change your grades. The following three concepts, when adopted into your learning habits, are proven to boost your long-term learning.

HOW

Although the structure and grading systems of most schools go counter to these concepts, you can still incorporate them into your study habits. Because the Academic Life Coaching Program is a *life coaching* program, it is important that the information about learning styles is assimilated into action as well as designed jointly by you and your coach. Your Academic Life Coach will have some specific suggestions for how to best integrate learning styles into a study method. However, it is up to you to co-design the exercises to build your learning styles, as well as integrate them into your study habits with your coach. Those three concepts are:

1. **Self-Quiz**

    Asking yourself to recall information, also referred to as retrieval, is the key to long-term learning. Self-quizzes, or tests, are most useful at the very beginning and midway through the learning process. Unfortunately, most tests are given at the end of the process to see how much a student has learned. This is the least effective place for a test. Putting in effort at the beginning of a concept is absolutely key to committing concept to your long-term memory. To further cement that concept in long-term memory, it is important to test yourself and the information you have learned. The Academic Life Coaching Program uses the Academic Thinking Styles as a way to organize and test your knowledge of a subject. Testing yourself on the definition, reason, and sequence of each concept mid-way through the learning process is ideal for long-term learning.

2. **Engage Multiple Senses**

    The pervasive myth of learning styles is that if you are taught in your preferred learning style (visual, audio, kinesthetic or VAK) then you will learn the information better. Many scientific studies have shown that matching instruction to a preferred style simply does not provide any boost to long-term memory or learning. However, engaging all of your senses, especially using imagery, visual, or audio memory cues to create a mental map of the concept, has been proven to boost long-term memory.

3. Short, Frequent Study Sessions

Effort helps long-term learning. Repeating the same concept in rapid succession might seem like you are learning because you can repeat what you just read, but that kind of massed learning (commonly referred to as cramming) is nearly useless in the long-run. The ideal learning condition is a series of practice sessions spaced out just to the point where it takes some effort to work through the solution or remember the concept from the previous practice session. The process of retrieving fuzzy information from yesterday might feel like more work and be less encouraging, but in the long-run, that effort cements long-term learning.

Recipe for Academic Success

In the business world, executives spend a great deal of time and energy identifying what's known as Key Performance Indicators or KPIs. Knowing what moves the dial and what differentiates the signal from the noise can make a huge difference in your success. Consider your Recipe for Academic Success as your search for your personal and academic KPIs.

WHAT

Recipe for Academic Success is a quick check in to make sure that you're doing what you need to do to succeed academically. If you are not getting the grades you want, or you are stressed out trying to get those grades, you are most likely not doing one of the following actions:

- **Using the three Science of Learning concepts:**

  - Self-quiz

  - Engaging the senses

  - Short, frequent study sessions

- **Applying the three Academic Thinking Styles to your studying.**

- **Using your planner and systems binder.**

- **Talking to your professor or teacher's assistant about what you can do better.**

WHY

The common thread through each of these actions is your worldview and orientation toward accomplishing what you want in your life. The more proactive you are and the more you care about what you're actually learning, the more successful you'll be. People like what they understand. If there's a challenging course or a class that's frustrating, taking steps to understand the material, connecting with the professor or TA, and getting on top of your homework adds a tremendous boost to your chances of actually liking your courses. And sometimes, you just have to grit it out. Either way, knowing your personal recipe helps you stay focused on actions that matter.

HOW

The process starts with a self-assessment to determine how well you are following through on each of the elements. A key point here is to balance a focus on the actual action steps and create a plan while also learning about yourself, your motivation, and the systems you have in place. Your performance offers valuable feedback and clues about how well you're doing, your weaknesses, and your strengths. As you craft your recipe and see how it impact your grades, you'll have an opportunity to continue to refine your studying based on the feedback you receive.

Questions to Consider:

1. **How are you doing with this list?**

2. **What action do you want to focus on first? When will you work on it?**

3. **How will you know that your action is contributing to your success?**

4. What other area in your life have you experienced success?

5. What made success easy for you?

6. How can you incorporate the same values/beliefs/actions to how you approach school and your grades?

Systems

Mindfully designing systems that support the habits you want to create is one of the keys to your success in college. When you're stressed out and wondering what you can do to relieve the stress while still getting the necessary work accomplished, working on your systems is a great use of your time and energy.

WHAT

A system has three parts. The first is the raw ingredients, or the starting point. It's what you have to work with, including your time and energy as well as your planner and other tangible structures you have in place. The second is the work flow that naturally happens based on the tools you have created to keep you organized and focused. The third is the final outcome of the process you've put in place.

WHY

Without a system, most people bounce between being completely on top of things (like having a clean room, an organized binder, and all their work finished) to being behind and failing to tame the homework monster (a messy room, a stuffed binder, and a few missing assignments). With a system there are sure to be times when things get hectic, but you are able to handle a bigger workload and more easily manage stress.

HOW

The best way to accomplish such an undertaking is by creating a system that is sustainable and designed to fit you. The key is to develop the system first, then do the work. The mistake most students make is diving into completing the work without thinking about what will work best in the future or designing a way to stay on top of the work.

Questions to Consider:

1. **What is your desired outcome?**

2. **What are the inputs or raw ingredients?**

3. **What is the natural flow that you want to see happen?**

4. **What structures do you need to put in place to be organized?**

5. **What are the decision points (those points in time when you have a choice to follow through with the system or do something else)?**

6. **What do you need to remind you to follow through?**

7. **What is currently working? (This gives you great clues about what you can build on.)**

8. **What is NOT currently working? (This gives you great clues about the structures you need.)**

Values

When you're working hard yet still feeling dissatisfied, working with a coach on clarifying values might be the exercise for you. When values aren't being honored, life can feel like chasing after something that never quite satisfies and leaves you feeling like you'll never be good enough. Taking a look at and aligning actions with values requires courage. Coaching excels at exploring values and looking at what systems and actions will lead to fulfillment.

WHAT

Values are the clarification of a cherished belief or experience. At their best, values name an aspect of experience you enjoy. For example, the value "Red Boots" could refer to that specific experience of the moment when recognize you're making a brave choice and taking bold action.

WHY

Clarifying what's important to you helps you identify the most important action steps you can take. When you start taking the most important action steps, you experience a state of doing your life's most important work. Pursuing meaningful work is a path to satisfaction and happiness.

HOW

Your coach will lead you through a series of questions guided by the coach's natural curiosity. Your coach will listen deeply and ask inquisitive questions designed for you to explore what's truly important to you. When you start questioning assumptions you've held for years and allow yourself to dream, you may surprise yourself with what insights you can create.

Making Decisions

Now it is time to put your values into action, especially when it comes time for you to make decisions. To make informed decisions, you have to know what's most important to you. Your values can help guide decisions, especially when you identify what is most important to you and decide to consciously include more of it in your life.

WHAT

Making Decisions is an exercise that builds on two concepts: Values and Systems. A system has inputs, a process, and a result. Making Decisions helps you visualize that process and the exact moment when you decide to follow through and honor your value, or you let the moment pass.

WHY

When you start to visualize and plan to create structures, you break down a larger problem, such as putting together a thesis. This helps you break the problem into smaller, more manageable steps. When you apply the insights and knowledge you gain from a coaching session to the process, you start to leverage all the inner work you are doing.

HOW

The first step in the process is to identify the value or system you want to use. From there, you look at the situation you want to apply the insight to and the process you want to put in place. You then have an opportunity to explore the exact decision point in your life where you take your life's most meaningful action steps. As you continue to develop more systems, you'll find yourself crafting ever-evolving systems which quickly become habits and the bedrock of your success.

Values

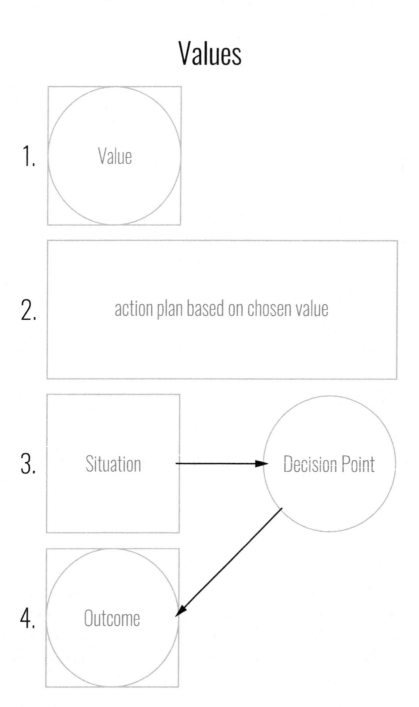

Identifying Your Passions

Identifying Passions, as a life coaching exercise, is a lot like turning over rocks to see if you find anything interesting. So many times people neglect or dismiss interests or think that pursuing passions can't possibly lead to a sustainable career. In fact, identifying what you truly like to do is the best way to find meaningful work that you excel at doing.

WHAT

A passion is a specific activity you love to do. It could be playing chess or it could be designing clothing or writing reviews of shoes. We live in a world where technology gives us the power to follow interests and create value by sharing insights with others. A passion is something you care so much about that pursuing it isn't work as much as a super-charged interest.

WHY

Many people have learned to turn off passions because at some point someone said you can't make money spending your time pursuing what you love. However, with so many career options available, your ability to become an effective and fulfilled adult relies on knowing yourself and how you best fit with the world. Coaching is excellently designed to help you explore and clarify your passions. Identifying Passions is a core life coaching concept.

HOW

In this session, you are invited to explore what you love. The next step is to follow it, design a way that you can act now to nurture your passion, and see its impact on your community.

Questions to Consider:

1. What do you love to do?

2. If you had two weeks completely free, what would you pursue?

3. Is there anything odd that you are interested in that most of your friends are not?

4. What would you love to pursue as a career?

Mission Statement

When you're searching for a foundation for your work, creating a mission statement is the exercise for you. A mission statement gives tangibility to your passion and a focus to your energy.

WHAT

A mission statement is a sentence that describes what you want to achieve, its purpose, and its larger meaning. It's an expression of the intersection of your passion, any need you see in the world, and the calling you feel in your heart.

In this exercise, you will find your mission statement by using a Venn diagram. The first circle is what your heart yearns for. What are you called to do? The second circle is what your community or what the world is yearning for. What does the world need? What service is the world asking for? The intersection of these two desires is where your leadership thrives.

WHY

Creating a mission statement takes creativity, imagination, and work. The effort to create a mission statement delivers as much benefit as having one to guide future actions.

A mission statement gains power when it both aligns with a passion as well as a need in the world. It's at the intersection of these two elements that magic happens.

HOW

Start with what you're passionate about. What do you feel fired up to achieve? What is your heart calling you to do? Then, move to what is needed in the world. Your coach will guide you through the process of exploring each area as well as the intersection between the two.

Mission Statement

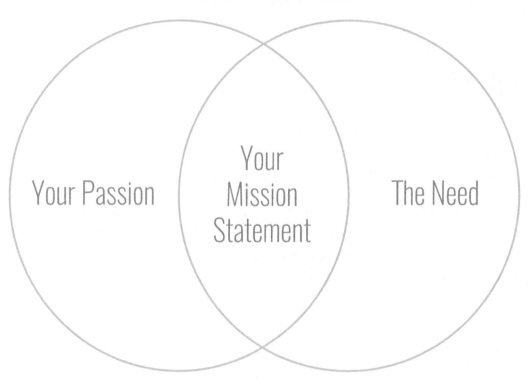

Leadership Projects

Mission statements give your project a focus. A Leadership Project makes your passion and mission statement tangible. The length of a leadership project can vary widely; from a weekend, to a decade, to a lifetime.

WHAT

A leadership project can be short, like helping plan a family vacation that includes meaningful time together, or take a lifetime, like building a business or trying to change the world in a meaningful way. Other projects could last months, like an internship. Along the way, your mission statement creates a frame for your leadership project just as your project produced tangible results from your mission statement. The two go hand-in-hand.

WHY

The quality of the leadership project you choose to undertake determines the quality of the leader you become. If you want to grow yourself personally and professionally, choose an ambitious project. The requirements of the project will show you where your blind spots are. It will grow you in unexpected and beautiful ways. When you start to do your life's work and serve others, the fulfillment will far outpace the inevitable challenges. Indeed, the challenges and the pain will become cherished parts of your journey. With the support of your coach, you have a powerful ally to help you craft and start to execute your vision.

HOW

The first step is to look for what is needed in your community and determine the impact you want to have on the lives of others. Your coach will lead you through the following prompts to explore different aspects; from the mission and scope of the project, to perspectives and action steps you want to take.

1. **What is needed in your community?**

2. **If your life were thriving, what gift or service would you offer others?**

3. **If you were to accomplish your leadership project, what would be the benefit in the lives of others?**

The second step is to revisit your mission statement and determine what project—it may be only a few weeks or it may span a few years—addresses that need in your community and aligns with your mission.

Brainstorm possible projects:

Circle the top 2

Name of project:

Time frame:

Purpose: Why this, why now?

Break down the larger project into smaller segments:

1st Well-Designed Action:

2nd Well-Designed Action:

3rd Well-Designed Action:

Possible adjustments you will need to make:

Name of project:

Time frame:

Purpose: Why this, why now?

Break down the larger project into smaller segments:

1st Well-Designed Action:

2nd Well-Designed Action:

3rd Well-Designed Action:

Possible adjustments you will need to make:

Leadership Styles with Core Motivation

When you start stepping up into a position of leadership, it's useful to know your natural leadership strengths and possible blind spots. This short but effective table offers some insight that builds off of the Core Motivation Tool found earlier in the program.

WHAT

The Leadership Styles tool is a way of using the Core Motivation tool to understand yourself better as a leader. Core Motivation comprises nine different personality types with certain strengths and weaknesses. In the table that follows, the left column details usual challenges to effective leadership that each type faces. The right column looks at what usually happens when you tap into your natural strengths.

WHY

Understanding yourself is a huge asset when trying to accomplish a project. If you're after a leadership project or looking at graduate school or beyond, using the Core Motivation Tool to gain a deeper understanding of yourself leverages all the inner work you've done. Once you do your inner work, the outer results will follow.

HOW

Read the columns that correspond to your Core Motivation Type and ask yourself what applies and what doesn't. Use it as a launching point of discussion in your session with your coach.

Challenges to Effective Leadership	When I tap into my natural leadership styles
Type 1: The Perfectionist	
Mistakes, errors. Pressure of having so many things to get right. Not being able to stop thinking if what I am doing is good enough. Others blaming me.	When I allow myself to have fun and enjoy. When I accept myself and the situation as it is.
Type 2: The Helper	
Others not recognizing me. Having too much to do for others and not having time for myself. Caring too much about relationships.	When I don't depend on the recognition of others. When I focus on action that is also beneficial for myself as well as others.
Type 3: The Doer	
Others thinking poorly of me. Inefficiency: things getting in the way of accomplishing a goal. Pressure from ambitious goals.	When I allow myself to focus on fulfillment. When I set aside the desire to look good for the sake of accomplishing a meaningful goal.
Type 4: The Artist	
When others do not acknowledge how I'm feeling, or even worse, when they tell me not to feel that way. Feeling inadequate, abandoned.	When I embrace the ordinary and work to make it exceptional. When I focus on principles without getting sidetracked by emotions.
Type 5: The Thinker	
Demands on my time and energy. People invading my space. Being proven factually wrong.	When I take action and connect with people. Thoughtful and astute, as a Type 5, I have the ability to think deeply about problems and create lasting solutions.
Type 6: The Friend	

Danger or threats. Not trusting other people. People breaking their promises or being unreliable. Dwelling on problems.	As Type 6, I am magnetic when I focus on positive goals and view problems as challenges and opportunities. When I act on positive assumptions.
Type 7: The Optimist	
Thinking that something better is out there for me. Feeling trapped in something boring or painful. Too many options, not enough time or limits on getting what I want.	As Type 7, I can use my natural ability to stir things up for a purpose. When I am willing to face negative situations and emotions and stay focused on creating positive outcomes.
Type 8: The Defender	
People who take advantage of me or others. Weakness in myself and others. Stupidity. Unfairness. When I sense injustice.	As Type 8, I usually have a big impact. As a natural leader, I truly shine when I take other people's needs and feelings into account.
Type 9: The Peacemaker	
Having people angry at me. Going along with the plans of others, even if I don't agree with them. Not being able to say no. Seeing possible problems but ignoring them.	When I have a clearly defined goal and I'm willing to step outside my comfort zone to take measured steps to accomplish goals.

Motivation Styles

Life coaching is designed to get you moving into action. Much of the magic in coaching comes from sparking motivation to change processes for the better. Harnessing motivation can be a challenge, but it is also one of the key skills for you to master in leading an effective life.

WHAT

The Academic Life Coaching Program looks at three distinctions in motivation styles to give you a better understanding of the factors of motivation and a specific mix that works best for you.

Those three distinctions are:

- **Conditional vs. Intrinsic**

- **Reactive vs. Proactive**

- **Sake of Self vs. Others**

Understanding the different motivation styles gives you a more specific vocabulary to gain a deeper insight into what really motivates you.

WHY

The purpose of this section is to help you become more aware of the kinds of motivation available as well as the characteristics, strengths, and weaknesses of each type of motivation.

Every style is useful. However, given different circumstances, some of these styles are going to be more useful to you than others. Once you are more aware of the different kinds and styles of motivation, you can more consciously tap into those that work best at different times for different projects.

HOW

By exploring the effect of different motivation styles at different times, you will gain familiarity with each style's different feel. You are literally developing your Emotional Intelligence, especially self-awareness and self-control. Misunderstanding the benefits and drawbacks of each kind of motivation is a large reason why many people have a hard time being productive and proactive instead of procrastinating.

As a student, the habits you set now will be your default habits of motivation throughout the rest of your life. By establishing habits of motivation mindfully, and experiencing that joy of being on top of your work and ahead of schedule, you are setting yourself up for a positive spiral of motivation and accomplishment. These feelings set the stage for flow.

Conditional vs. Intrinsic Motivation

WHAT

Conditional motivation is being motivated to do something for the sake of an external benefit. It is when people think, "If I do this, then I get this reward." Or it could be "If I don't do this, this won't happen." Anytime someone uses a conditional sentence—a pair of *if-then* clauses—he or she is using conditional motivation.

Intrinsic motivation is being motivated to do something because the action itself is the reward. It is when someone thinks, "I want to do this because it's fun." Or it could be, "I enjoy the challenge." Or even, "I want to see what happens when I follow through with..." Intrinsic motivation is about enjoying the process as much as the result.

While conditional motivation works well in the short-term, to be successful in school without all the stress, it is important to find a way to be intrinsically motivated. In other words, you must find a way to balance doing your homework for the sake of the grade with doing your homework because learning and doing the work is enjoyable.

WHY

We've all had the experience of being on top of your work or doing an assignment and actually enjoying it. It is natural, *the brain wants to learn*. Finding that place where learning is fun allows you to take more control of your motivation so you can switch at-will between conditional (for short bursts of energy) and intrinsic (your main engine).

HOW

The biggest key in shifting to intrinsic motivation, which will be more useful in the long-run, is simply being aware of which motivation style you are using. Self-awareness goes a long way to determining which style you use. Once you find the joy of tapping into an intrinsic style of motivation, it can quickly become a positive habit.

Questions to Consider:

1. **When do you find yourself using conditional motivation?**

2. **What work do you do for the fun of it?**

3. **When do you catch yourself having fun five minutes after starting something hard?**

4. **If you were in a sweet office with other people working nearby and had to produce something by the end of the weekend, what would you produce?**

5. **In your school work, how often do you motivate yourself with rewards?**

6. **What is your ideal balance between conditional and intrinsic motivation?**

Reactive vs. Proactive Motivation

WHAT

Motivation works both ways. You can either move towards what you want, called toward or proactive motivation. Or you can move away from what you don't want, called away from or reactive motivation. Both forms of motivation have positive and negative aspects to them. For instance, if there is an emergency, reactive motivation is a powerful tool to marshal resources and respond very quickly.

WHY

We all use both forms of motivation every day. Each style has useful and useless aspects to it. Reactive motivation is useful in short spurts but tends to flame out. Proactive motivation is hard to spark, but once lit, it is a powerful force. Understanding your mix of motivation and having an insight into how to use each of these types at different times, for different purposes, gives you an advantage in completing meaningful work.

How

Consider the following charts and your pattern in looking at doing meaningful work. The first chart below is an example of being motivated AWAY from what you don't want, which could be a bad grade or not getting that internship. The second chart demonstrates a motivation towards pattern. It's much harder to get going, but once you get rolling, the speed and motivation pick up. Your coach will help you explore both styles and craft action steps and systems that help you tap into both.

Questions to consider:

1. **In school, what is your usual balance between being motivated 'away from' vs. 'towards'?**

2. **What areas of your life do you find yourself using an 'away from' motivation style?**

3. **What areas of your life do you find yourself using a 'towards' motivation style?**

This chart below is an example of being motivated *away* from what you don't want to happen. You can imagine that whenever performance dips below a certain point, panic sets in and we start to sprint and do whatever we can to get back to a comfortable place. The challenge becomes the yo-yo effect of constantly sprinting, then relaxing. In short bursts, motivation away from is useful. Over the long-run, it tends to be exhausting.

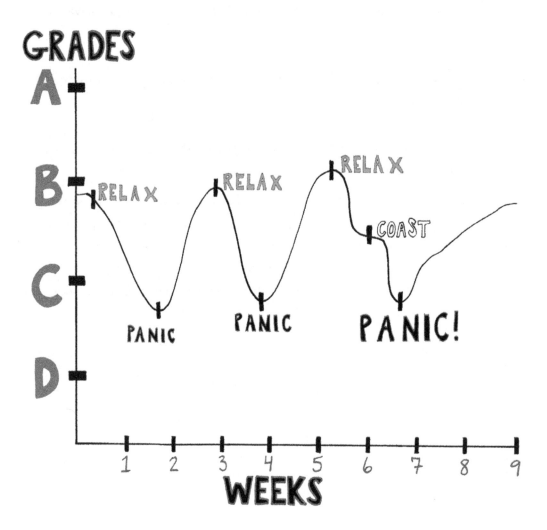

The chart below is an example of being motivated toward what you *do* want to happen. Notice how it may be difficult to get moving at first because you are so far away from your primary source of motivation. Once you get closer to the outcome you want, you start to pick up the pace because you can see how close you are and getting what you want becomes real and achievable.

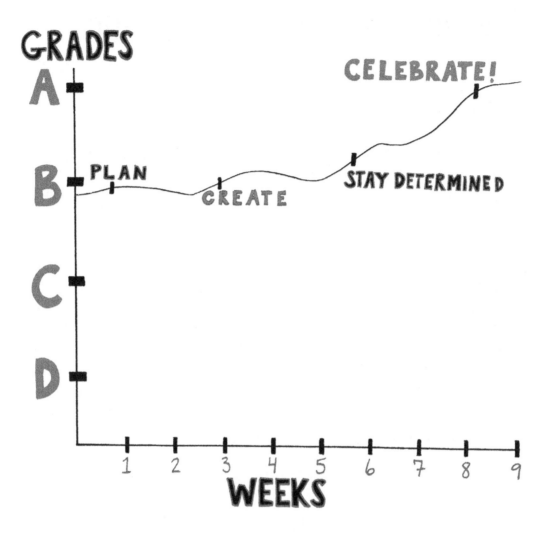

Sake of Self vs. Other Motivation

WHAT

There is a vast difference between being motivated for the sake of yourself and for the sake of others, yet the distinction goes unaddressed for most of your academic career. Motivation for the sake of self can be exhilarating, but it's not nearly as fulfilling and exciting as doing something for the sake of others.

WHY

So much of the culture surrounding young people is designed to create a sense of entitlement and self-focus. "What do you want to do when you grow up?" "What's your interest?" From advertisers trying to sell you more stuff, to a school culture detached from practical application, understanding what you want to do with your life is a complex maze. Exploring sake-of-self versus sake-of-other motivation helps you navigate both your immediate challenges and the first steps in your career.

HOW

In the following section, you'll see a chart that allows you to explore the difference between the two kinds of motivation. In a combination with reactive and proactive motivation, you have a chart to explore the different perspectives and energy each area offers.

Action to take:

	Skipped it	Did it
In my life		
In the lives of others (parents or friends)		
In the future (in the lives of people you do not yet know.)		

Assumption Chart

When you have a suspicion that your mindset and self-talk is getting in the way, it's time to do an Assumption Chart.

WHAT

The Assumption Chart is really two charts. The first is the cycle you set off when you consciously or unconsciously make disempowering assumptions. The second covers the cycle of making empowering assumptions. Same chart, two cycles.

WHY

The recognition of the negative cycles brings so much clarity that it leads to useful insights allowing you to take different actions and engage in a different kind of self-talk.

HOW

Start with the negative assumption chart first. Really dig down to your most negative assumptions. Your coach will help you explore the negative cycle thoroughly, pull you out of the negativity, and then explore you positive and empowering assumption cycle.

Negative Assumption

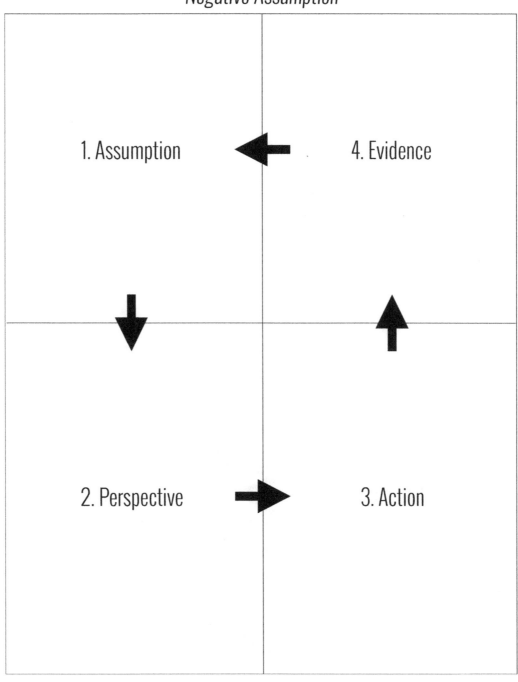

Positive Assumption

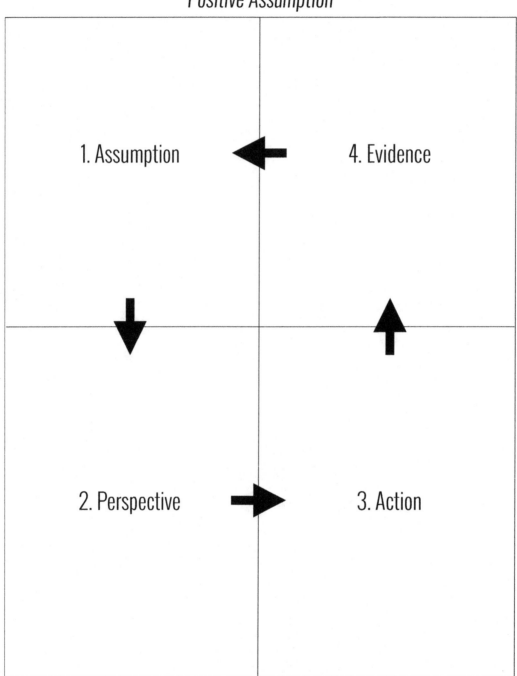

Busting Limiting Beliefs

At times throughout your coaching session, you'll have a coach question and push at different beliefs and assumptions you are making. When you want to do a more thorough exploration of possible beliefs holding you back, this exercise is for you.

WHAT

Busting Liming Beliefs is a quick exercise designed to get you to assess the main ideas you have about yourself and a project. The elements are: the original beliefs, a process to look at the opposite of those beliefs, and an outcome, which usually falls somewhere between the original and wildly different belief.

WHY

Limiting beliefs are easy to bust when you get into the habit of recognizing them. The key is to recognize areas where you are struggling, and determine what underlying beliefs you have about yourself or the tasks. Identify the beliefs that are limiting you. Once identified, you can use this Busting Limiting Beliefs exercise – or the assumptions chart – to realign your beliefs to best serve you.

HOW

It may be a stretch for you to switch to the opposite of a limiting belief, but when you choose an empowering belief, you start to look for evidence to support it. Your ability to build on what is working is a great skill to have in your tool belt. The process starts with listing your beliefs about yourself or an area of your life, and finishes with applying the new insights to an action step to experiment and play with.

Busting Limiting Beliefs

Challenge:

Negative Beliefs About Yourself	Helpful Beliefs About Yourself/Tasks

Past Actions	New Actions

Circle helpful beliefs

Cross out limiting beliefs

Write out what different actions you would take based on the positive beliefs you wrote above.

Perspectives

Sometimes, a small shift in perspective can make all the difference. Perspective is one of life coaching's core exercises and is woven through many of the other exercises you will do with your coach.

WHAT

Perspective is an exercise designed to lead you through exploring your starting perspective, a handful of other perspectives, and action steps based on your most empowered perspective.

WHY

Perspectives have a big impact on the quality of the action you take. A dire perspective leads to hasty action. A playful perspective leads to more energetic action. An empowering perspective leads to empowered action. Perspectives are engrained in how you see the world, and by making them conscious and designed, you are determining which perspective you want to operate from.

HOW

Your coach will help you start with a default perspective, create an emotionally neutral way to describe the situation, and then explore a handful of other perspectives. After you've determined which perspective you want to use, you'll have a chance to design your action steps for the next week or two.

Perspectives

1. starting situation

2. emotion-neutral way to describe situation

3. default perspective

another perspective

another perspective

another perspective

4.   Highlight the perspective you want to use.

5.   Action plan based on that perspective

Vision Recording

When you want to supercharge your motivation, creating a Vision Recording is the perfect exercise. You gain as much benefit from creating the recording as you do listening to it over the weeks and months to come.

WHAT

Simple, powerful, and elegant, a Vision Recording is a 2 to 5-minute recording of you painting a picture of what your life will be like at some point in the future. Add music to the background of your recording, and you add a powerful tool to your motivational tool belt.

WHY

Your vision recording should remind you of an outcome you are striving for to make it easier for you to tap into proactive motivation (instead of reactive motivation). Your recording can be used to remind you of the actions that you want to take or habits that you want to build. It works because it is easy to press the play button, sit back, and soak in the positive energy from your recording.

HOW

Your coach will guide you through the goals you have for the next three months, the actions and habits that you will need to take and develop to get there, and what you will see, hear, and feel once you step into that reality.

Your coach will also help you put together a plan to make your recording. Most people use Garage Band or a similar app to lay a track of voice over a song.

Future Pacing

The Future Pacing exercise gives you a little pick-me-up and an extra boost of mojo.

WHAT

This is a type of visualization exercise where you imagine yourself taking the steps you most want and need to take in the near future.

WHY

When you visualize yourself doing the action, you increase your chances of actually following through. Visualization is a powerful tool to help your mind and body prepare for a future challenge.

HOW

Your coach will lead you through an exercise where you create a future scenario with as much detail as possible about what it will be like to take an important action step.

Questions to Consider:

1. **When you put yourself in the future, what's the most important step ahead of you?**

2. **What happens when you make the choice you really want to make?**

3. **What would change in other areas of your life?**

4. What do you hope to learn about yourself?

Self-Alignment: Getting Over Jetlag

This exercise is like taking yourself to the chiropractor. You have to get realigned every so often, especially when you're making the kind of big changes that you have been making over the past few weeks. Just like jetlag, the understanding you have of yourself and the insights you've experienced have moved you to a different place relatively quickly. This exercise aims to help the rest of your life catch up to that new place.

WHAT

This is a short and quick exercise that can lead to deep insights. The exercise uses an assessment wheel and applies insights you have in one area of your life to other areas.

WHY

So much of life coaching depends on temporarily suspending attachment to a problem, exploring different perspectives and avenues of thought, and then going back to that original perspective. This exercise mimics that process. As you take an insight from one area and apply it to different areas, you both refine the original insight and break new ground in other areas of your life.

HOW

Start with a recent insight, perspective, or value you've created with your coach. Use the *Wheel of Life* to take that value and apply it to a different area. Sometimes the insight makes sense and other times it falls flat. Either way, precious nuggets of understanding are unearthed in the process.

Wheel of Life

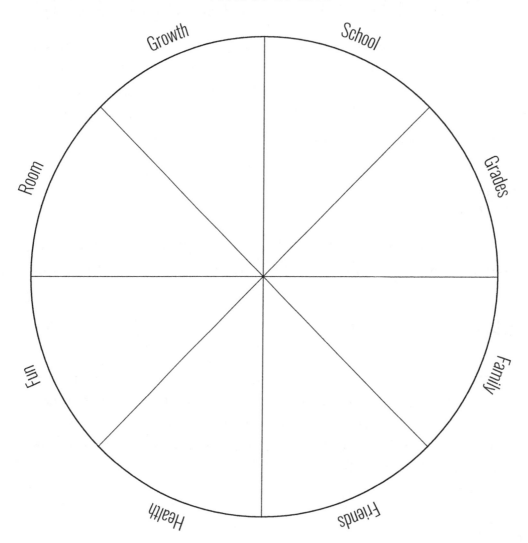

Future-Self

The Future-Self is one of the Wellness Coach Training Program's most popular exercises. It's an exercise that invites you to explore a powerful future perspective and compare it to the present moment. It's useful for when you need clarity and guidance in making important decisions and reaching the next level.

What

The Future-Self is an exercise designed to get you to create an accurate picture of yourself 10 years in the future. Essentially, the Future-Self exercise is a designed perspective of a positive version of yourself one decade into the future.

Why

Research has shown that simply thinking about a positive "possible self" in the future has a positive impact on well-being (Markus & Nurius 1986, King 2001).

How

Your coach will guide you through a 10-minute visualization for you to "meet" your Future-Self. From there, your coach will take you through a series of questions to explore this powerful perspective and tool.

Questions to Consider:

1. **What is your future-self's nickname?**

2. **Fashion style?**

3. Where does your future-self live?

4. What is your future-self's home like?

5. What's a typical day for your future-self?

6. When do you need your future-self's message the most?

7. What would you like to say to your future-self?

8. What are your future-self's top values?

9. What is your future-self's message to you?

Inner-Critic

The Inner Critic Exercise is a fantastic exercise to use when you feel like you're being too hard on yourself or when negative self-talk is getting in the way.

What

Your inner-critic is the negative self-talk, images, and feelings that make up your internal dialogue. In this exercise, you will use your imagination to separate yourself from this not-so-helpful voice.

Why

This exercise helps you create distance between you and negative self-talk. Once you create a little distance, you increase your chances of being able to respond from a more empowered perspective.

How

The first step is to look at what kinds of things you say to yourself when things are going well. The next step is to gain clarity on negative self-talk. Your coach will lead you through an exercise to gain clarity on the negative self-talk and create a small cartoon-like figure to represent your inner critic. From there, you get to design a new job description and method for dealing with your critic when he or she pops up.

Questions to Consider:

1. **What kinds of things do you say to yourself when you're doing poorly?**

2. If you were to imagine someone else saying this to you, who/what would it look like?

3. What would its name be?

4. How big or small?

5. Other physical description (for example, what kind of clothes does your critic wear?)

6. What is its mission?

7. When does it show up most often?

8. What would its biography be?

Setting a Reminder

Once you've done all this hard work with your coach, setting a reminder to use coaching concepts throughout the day gives you an added boost.

What

The Setting a Reminder Exercise is a simple association. It's linking a specific concept, such as Perspective or Value, to a hand movement or essential oil scent. A reminder can be used to create a deeper sense of peace and gratitude. A reminder can be used to boost motivation and energy.

Why

The connection between mind and body is powerful. Once you establish a link between a concept and a movement or scent, you've created a useful tool to recall the concept to mind throughout a busy day.

How

The first step is to get clear on what exactly you want to be reminded of. Your coach will lead you through both parts of the exercise as well as help you design when and how you're going to use your reminder.

Questions to Consider:

1. **What perspective or value do you want to be reminded of?**

2. **How would a reminder impact your decision?**

3.   **What impact would different action steps have on your life?**

Assumptions in Relationships

Relationships are central to living a fulfilling life. This exercise helps you take an important look at relationships to ensure you're aligning your assumptions with your actions to build the relationship you want.

WHAT

The Assumptions in Relationships exercise is a journey in the exploration of the ideas you hold about yourself and the other person, the actions you take, and the impact those actions have on others. It's a chart that helps you visualize how your assumptions have an impact on their behavior and vice versa.

WHY

It's sometimes tough to see yourself. This exercise offers you the opportunity to take a step back and reevaluate how you want to be in relationship. It encourages you to assess whether or not you want to put in the work to help the relationship improve or explore how you want to protect yourself mentally and emotionally. When you start to look at the assumptions you are making in relationships, you empower yourself with the choice between which relationships to pour energy into and which relationships to simply manage.

HOW

Choose a relationship you want to spend time exploring. Look at how that relationship impacts your life. On the first of two charts, dive into the negative. Dig deep into the negative assumptions you have about the situation. Allow yourself to go negative. You'll have a chance to go super positive later and the distinction between how you feel will be instructive. Your coach will be able to guide you to deeper insights and an action plan on how you want to use what you've learned in the session.

Here is an opportunity for you to change your assumption, which will break the negative pattern and focus your attention on building the relationship.

Assumptions in Relationships

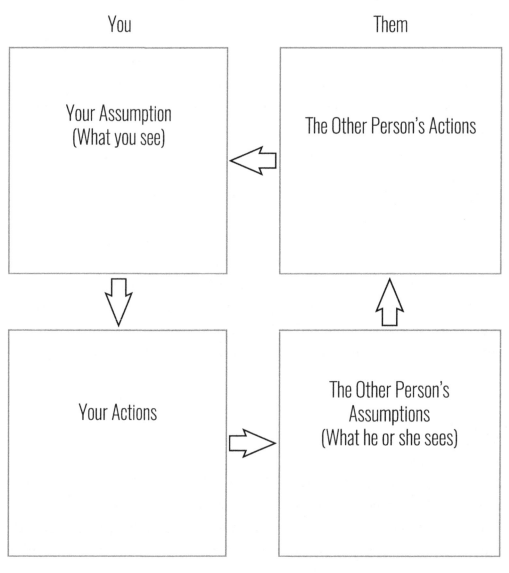

You

Them

Your Assumption
(What you see)

The Other Person's Actions

Your Actions

The Other Person's
Assumptions
(What he or she sees)

Building Empathy

Excellent communication is essential for a fulfilling life. One of the main ingredients of outstanding communication is empathy.

WHAT

Empathy is the ability to accurately imagine what another person is feeling and thinking and to see situations from their point-of-view.

- **Level 1 Communication is listening and speaking for the sake of yourself.**

- **Level 2 Communication is listening and speaking for the sake of another and imagining their experience *from their point-of-view*.**

WHY

Both levels of communication are necessary and valuable. Level one is not necessarily better or worse than level two, however, most people spend most of their time in level one. The worksheet below helps you practice level two communication and helps you further develop the important Emotional Intelligence skill of empathy.

HOW

Start with another person's name. Step into this person's point-of-view and imagine what their world would be like. Consider questions such as:

1. **What would be most important to them?**

2. **What are their biggest dreams, hopes, and fears?**

Stretch those empathetic muscles. Then apply the experience to another area in your life.

Completion

Congratulations on finishing the
Academic Life Coaching Program!

Throughout this program you have amassed an impressive set of tools to help you succeed academically, personally, and as a leader.

The program is cyclical. By going back through the exercises and comparing where you were when you went through the first time with how far you have come, you bring a new understanding for how you can bring all the parts of the program together. The power of the program is not in its one time application. These concepts are meant to be woven into your life so that you naturally live your life while being conscious of your values and the choices that you are making. You know how to choose a powerful perspective and recover to it when something knocks you off balance. You understand the importance of living with a mission and how exciting it is to start to see a leadership project become a reality.

You are invited to complete the next three exercises with your coach to complete your coaching relationship.

And I also invite you to continue your journey and to contribute to the Academic Life Coaching community online through our website and blog at academiclifecoaching.com. The more people in this community moving forward, the stronger the tide, and the more everyone benefits.

Designing the Future

Consider the Designing the Future exercise Leadership Project-lite. If you tackled the Leadership Project exercise early in your coaching, or if you're aiming to create a smaller project, then Design the Future is for you.

When your coaching relationship is coming to a close, it's time to take a look to the future. It's time to take wings and fly using all the concepts and insights you've gained through all of your coaching sessions.

WHAT

Designing the Future is an exercise that aims is to craft a future project that will help you continue the work that you've done with your coach. It's a simple exercise that taps into the ideas of growth mindset and practical application as a means of continuing personal, academic, and professional development.

WHY

School is often premised on developing the skill set first, then going out to find a project or do work that matches the skill set. It makes sense. But outside of school, when you're confronted by new projects and problems, your ability to learn on the fly and apply all of the coaching concepts, makes the difference in your success. This exercise helps you mindfully design the next chapter with your coach as you complete your coaching relationship.

HOW

After celebration comes the work of getting to the next level. Incorporating your recent successes—and imagining a new set of successes in the coming year—creates a vision for yourself a year from now. From that point in the future, look back on what you have accomplished.

Capture that vision, either in a sound recording or by drawing it out on paper. Then listen to your recording or post the drawing in a place you will often see it. The more you tap into that vision and take action steps, the more effective and fulfilled your life can be.

Resilience

Throughout the course of being coached, you've had an opportunity to experience setbacks but also experience recovery. Along the way, you've learned about yourself and established systems to help move you forward. This exercise is about helping you capture all of that learning and create a plan of action for when you experience future setbacks.

WHAT

Resilience is expecting that things won't always work out and creating contingency plans to get back on track. A complete plan addresses both the internal world, for example specific perspectives and motivation styles, as well as external support, for example, who you can rely on to help keep you accountable.

WHY

Research has shown that the most resilient people are those who have an optimistic view of their potential and ability but a pessimistic view of the challenges. When you consider the challenges to be tough, you're more likely to persist and try new things without judging yourself to be unworthy. The thinking goes something like this: since the challenge is so hard, of course it's going to take more time and effort to be successful. Add to that mindset a plan of action, and you dramatically increase your chances of being successful.

HOW

The more you learn to recover from setbacks and build up your resilience the better leader you will be. The aim here is to cut down the amount of time it takes for you to recover. You are at a point now where you have many tools to help you do that. This exercise is about finding the perspectives, values, and motivation to build your resilience.

Questions to Consider:

1. **What tools (perspectives, values, future-self, etc.) have worked well for you over the past three months?**

2. **What systems have worked well over the past 3 months?**

3. **Within those systems, what key structures have you put in place?**

4. **What are some examples of when you have recovered quickly?**

5. **How did you recover in the past?**

6. **Why did it work so well?**

7. **How would you like to recover in the future?**

8. **What did you learn about yourself when you recovered?**

9. **Who could you reach out to when needed?**

10. **How does this plan interact with your future projects?**

Celebration

It is important to take time to celebrate success. In the fast pace of contemporary life, successes quickly become a part of the past in the drive to accomplish even more.

WHAT

Celebration is an opportunity to look back over the past few months to celebrate your achievements. It's an artform as well as an acknowledgement of all the hard work you've put into your personal growth.

WHY

Celebrating successes reinforces and reminds you that hard work pays off and that playing the long game is worth it. When you start to do important, meaningful work within the structure of a coaching relationship, Celebration becomes a reminder for you in the future that doing the hard work is really worth it.

HOW

Your coach will lead you through exploring different successes you've experienced over the past few months. You can also start with doing another wheel of life to see how far you've come and how much the coaching has had an impact on your life. Then you get to plan a celebration. It can either be an experience to remember or something you acquire to remind yourself of how hard work pays off.

In this wheel, write your current level of satisfaction with each area of your life.

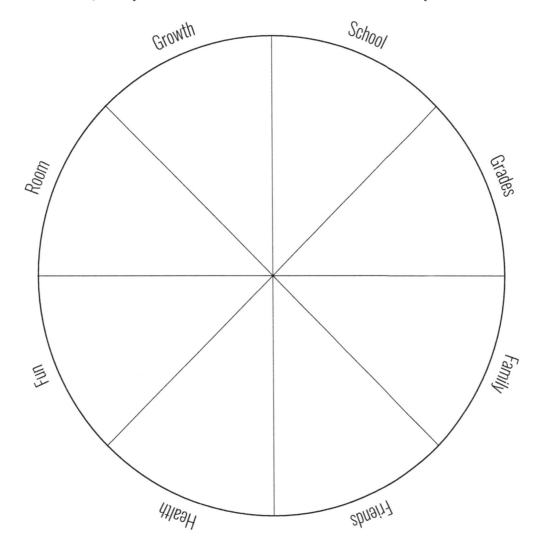

NOTES:

Made in the USA
Columbia, SC
08 December 2020